slow cooking

imagine THAT!™

Imagine That! is an imprint of Top That! Publishing plc,
Tide Mill Way, Woodbridge, Suffolk, IP12 IAP, UK
www.topthatpublishing.com
Copyright © 2009 Top That! Publishing plc
Imagine That! is a trademark of Top That! Publishing plc.

Contents

Contents

What is Slow Cooking?

Slow cooking is a fantastic way to prepare meals that are tender and full of flavour with hardly any effort! A great asset to the kitchen, slow cookers are ideal if you like a home-cooked meal but don't have much time to spare.

There are many benefits to slow cooking. Food cooked over a long period of time retains moisture and becomes softer and more absorbent – ideal if you want to use cheaper cuts of meat that are tough and unpopular for roasting or grilling. Many of the recipes in this flipover are slow cooked in 5+ hours – perfect for busy and hectic lifestyles.

Top Tip!
Many of the recipes suggest that the meat is browned before it is added to the slow cooker. This step isn't neccessary, however, browning adds colour and helps with the flavour development. Whilst you are browning the meat, start the slow cooker on a low heat with the lid on, so it will be warm when you add the ingredients.

Slow cooking was popularised in the 1970s and is still widely used today. Most slow cookers are round or oval in shape and are made from heat-resistant materials, saving energy and retaining nutrients.

What is Slow Cooking?

A variety of different meats, vegetables and pulses can be slow cooked, as long as they are covered in some sort of liquid (water, wine or stock), depending on the recipe. Cooking in plenty of liquid prevents the ingredients from drying out over the longer cooking time. (Depending on your slow cooker, you may need to adjust the amount of liquid used.)

The lid on the slow cooker not only prevents hot liquid from splashing, but it also forces the steam back to liquid, ensuring that the ingredients stay moist and full of flavour.

Top Tip!

Don't lift the lid to stir, unless the recipe specifies, especially if you are cooking on a low setting. Every time the lid is removed, heat will escape. This will result in an extended cooking time of 20–30 minutes.

Low High

Off Warm

Beef

With a great variety of cuts that are perfect for a longer cooking time, beef is one of the best meats for slow cooking and many delicious dishes can be made from even the cheapest cuts of meat. The most common and popular cuts of beef to use in a slow cooker include joints from the neck, shoulder and lower leg.

Hungarian Goulash

Hungarian Goulash

Hungarian goulash has been cooked for thousands of years. It was cooked as early as 800 A.D. using a large cauldron (a bográc in Hungarian) and cooked over an open fire.

You will need:

- 800 g (1 lb, 7 oz) braising or rump steak, cut into cubes
- 2 tablespoons plain flour
- 1 tablespoon oil
- 1 onion, chopped
- 1 clove garlic, crushed
- salt and pepper to season
- 1½ teaspoons paprika
- 1 teaspoon dried thyme, crushed
- 400 g (14 oz) canned chopped tomatoes
- beef stock cube, dissolved in a small amount of hot water
- 100 ml (3 fl. oz) red wine
- 250 ml (8 fl. oz) sour cream

Serves 4–5

1. Dust the pieces of beef lightly in plain flour, while you heat up a frying pan with some oil.

2. Brown the pieces of beef, a few at a time, so you don't drop the pan's temperature and end up cooking the beef rather than browning. Once browned, remove to a plate.

3. Add the beef to the slow cooker with the remaining ingredients, excluding the sour cream.

4. Stir well, cover and cook on high for 4–5 hours or on low for 8–10 hours.

5. In the last hour, remove the cover from the slow cooker. Continue to cook for the remaining time or until the sauce thickens. Add the sour cream 30 minutes before serving, and stir thoroughly.

Goulash can be served with any vegetables you fancy, or keep it simple with a portion of rice or noodles.

Beef in Red Wine Sauce

Beef in Red Wine Sauce

This succulent dish is perfect for long winter nights, curled up in front of an open fire. The red wine enhances the flavour of the beef and the dumplings are the perfect comfort food accompaniment.

You will need:

- 1 kg (2 lb, 2 oz) braising beef
- 2 tablespoons plain flour
- 2 tablespoons oil
- 1 onion, sliced finely
- 1 carrot, diced
- 2 cloves garlic, finely sliced
- 2 sticks of celery, stalks and leaves, finely sliced
- 1 tablespoon tomato purée
- salt and pepper to taste
- 375 ml (12 fl. oz) good red wine
- fresh parsley, roughly chopped

Dumplings (optional):
- 50 g (2 oz) suet
- 100 g (4 oz) plain flour
- ½ teaspoon baking powder
- pinch of salt
- 4–5 tablespoons cold water

Serves 6

1. First, prepare the beef by removing any sinew and excess fat, then cut into large chunks.

2. Dust the pieces of beef very lightly in plain flour while you heat up a frying pan with some oil.

3. Brown the pieces in the pan, a few at a time, so you don't drop the pan's temperature and end up cooking the beef, rather than browning. Once browned, remove to a plate.

4. When all of the meat is browned, add the onions, carrot, garlic and celery to the pan and sauté over a gentle heat for about 5 minutes so the vegetables absorb the pan flavours. Add the tomato purée and stir, then season with a little salt and pepper.

Beef in Red Wine Sauce

5. Next, add the beef to the slow cooker and any juices that have been released, then add the vegetable and tomato mixture, stirring thoroughly. Pour in the red wine so it covers the beef.

6. Cover and cook on high for 4–5 hours or on low for 8–10 hours.

7. For the dumplings, mix together the suet, flour, baking powder and salt. Add 4–5 tablespoons of cold water and mix until soft and slightly sticky. Roll into balls about the size of walnuts and remove to a plate.

8. In the last hour, remove the cover from the slow cooker and add the dumplings. Recover and continue to cook for the remaining time or until the sauce thickens. Stir from time to time if you need to.

9. During the last 5 minutes of cooking, stir in some freshly sliced parsley, and reserve some to garnish the final dish.

Serve with mashed potatoes and vegetables on a cold, winter evening.

Coconut Beef Madras

Coconut Beef Madras

Curries are great for slow cooking, as the spices and flavours deepen the longer the dish is cooked. This madras is sure to become a dinner party favourite!

You will need:

- 1.5 kg (3 lb, 3 oz) beef blade steak, cut into pieces
- 2 tablespoons plain flour
- 8 tablespoons vegetable oil
- 2 large onions, chopped
- 6 garlic cloves, crushed
- 5 cm (2 in.) ginger, finely chopped
- 4 tablespoons madras curry paste
- 200 ml (7 fl. oz) coconut milk
- 2 small cinnamon sticks
- 2 green chillies, halved lengthways
- 1 teaspoon salt

Serves 6

1. First, dust the steak very lightly in plain flour while you heat up a frying pan with some oil.

2. Brown the pieces, a few at a time, so you don't drop the pan's temperature and end up cooking the beef rather than browning. Once browned, remove to a plate.

3. Heat the rest of the oil, and add the onions, garlic and ginger. Fry gently for 20 minutes until very soft and light brown. Transfer to a food processor and blend until smooth.

4. Next, add the steak and the blended mixture to the slow cooker and add the curry paste, coconut milk, cinnamon sticks, chillies, and salt. Cover and cook on high for 4–5 hours or on low for 8–10 hours, uncovering for the last 15 minutes to thicken up the sauce a little.

5. Remove the cinnamon sticks and serve with steamed rice.

Beef Bourguignon

A traditional French recipe, beef bourguignon has become a classic for a good reason! It is an ideal slow cooking dish, as the ingredients fuse together to make a rich and flavoursome stew.

You will need:

- 100 g (4 oz) streaky bacon
- 1 tablespoon olive oil
- 900 g (2 lb) lean stewing steak, cut into cubes
- 340 g (12 oz) potatoes, sliced
- 1 sliced carrot
- 16 small onions or shallots, peeled
- 340 g (12 oz) button mushrooms
- salt and pepper to season
- 25 g (1 oz) plain flour
- 500 ml (17 fl. oz) red wine, Burgundy is good
- 250 ml (8 fl. oz) beef stock
- 1 tablespoon tomato purée
- 1 garlic clove, crushed
- ½ teaspoon thyme
- 1 bay leaf

Serves 4–6

1. Slice the streaky bacon into lengths. Heat up the olive oil in a frying pan and cook the bacon strips until lightly brown. Spoon them out (leaving as much oil remaining as possible) and set aside in a covered bowl.

2. Re-heat the remaining oil and bacon fat until it is very hot. Add the cubes of beef, in batches, and fry them until they are brown on all sides. Spoon these out and place in the bowl alongside the bacon.

3. Now, put the bacon and beef into the slow cooker and add the potatoes, sliced carrot, shallots and mushrooms. Season with salt and pepper and sprinkle with plain flour.

4. Stir in the red wine and enough beef stock to just cover the meat. Add the tomato purée, garlic and herbs. Cover and cook on low for 8–10 hours or on high for 4–5 hours.

Serve with green vegetables.

Top Tip!
To peel shallots quickly, place in a bowl and pour over boiling water. Leave for a few minutes, then drain, and the skins will slip off.

Oxtail Casserole

Oxtail Casserole

Oxtail is the tail meat from cattle and, when slow cooked, is one of the tastiest cuts of beef. Its soft, melting meat, teamed with this rich red wine sauce is perfect for parties.

You will need:

- 2 tablespoons plain flour
- salt and pepper to season
- 2 oxtails, jointed and cut into pieces
- 4 tablespoons oil
- 2 onions, chopped
- 3 carrots, cut into small chunks
- 2 celery sticks, cut into small chunks
- 2 garlic cloves, chopped
- 2 tablespoons tomato purée
- bay leaves and thyme sprigs, tied together
- 1 bottle full-bodied red wine
- 1 beef stock cube

Serves 6

1. Season the flour with salt and pepper, then toss the oxtail in it until it's evenly coated. Heat the oil in a large flameproof casserole dish. Working in batches, brown the meat well on all sides.

2. Remove from the pan and place into the slow cooker. Then, add the vegetables and garlic, and stir in the tomato purée and herbs.

3. Pour over the wine, then crumble in the stock cube. Season, cover and cook for 4–5 hours on high or 8–10 hours on low, until the meat is meltingly tender.

Serve with mashed potatoes and seasonal vegetables.

> **Top Tip!**
> This casserole can be cooked up to 2 days ahead. If you do make it ahead, chill in the fridge and lift any fat off the top before reheating.

Beef Brisket

Beef Brisket

Brisket is one of the cheapest and toughest cuts of beef. Despite this, slow cooking softens the cut and brings out its deep flavour, making beef brisket a hearty meal that melts in your mouth.

You will need:

- 50 g (2 oz) butter
- 1 kg (2 lb, 2 oz) fresh brisket of beef, rolled and tied
- 1 onion, quartered
- 2 large carrots, sliced
- 2 celery stalks, sliced
- 425 ml (14 fl. oz) beef stock
- $\frac{1}{2}$ teaspoon dried thyme
- $\frac{1}{2}$ teaspoon dried marjoram
- 1 tablespoon soy sauce
- salt and pepper to season
- 4 teaspoons cornflour

Serves 6

1. Melt the butter in a large saucepan and fry the brisket over a high heat until browned on all sides. Transfer to the slow cooker.

2. Add the onion, carrots and celery to the slow cooker, then add the stock, thyme, marjoram, soy sauce and freshly ground black pepper and salt to taste.

3. Cover and cook on high for 6–8 hours or on low for 8–9 hours, turning the meat over every 30 minutes.

4. When tender, remove the meat and vegetables from the pan and keep warm.

5. Blend the cornflour to a paste with a little cold water, stir into the cooker and cook on high for 2 minutes. Then, lower the heat and simmer for 2–3 minutes, stirring constantly.

6. Place the meat on a serving rack, cutting a few thin slices from one end. Pour over a little of the gravy, then serve at once, pouring the remaining gravy into a sauceboat.

Top Tip!
To turn the brisket over without splashing or burning yourself, use two large kitchen forks, or a fork and a wooden spoon. Make sure you have a firm grip on the joint before you lift it; if it slips back into the pan the hot stock will splash dangerously.

Steak and Stout Casserole

Steak and Stout Casserole

This is a soothing, comfortable plateful to drive out the chill of the coldest winter evening. The stout combined with the steak delivers a match made in heaven for your taste buds.

You will need:

- 1 tablespoon flour, seasoned with salt and pepper
- 900 g (2 lb) stewing beef, trimmed of fat and cubed
- 1 tablespoon oil
- 1 onion, sliced
- 450 ml (15 fl. oz) stout
- 200 ml (7 fl.oz) water / beef stock
- 2 bay leaves
- 225 g (8 oz) mushrooms, sliced
- 1 carrot, peeled and diced

Dumplings (optional):
- 50 g (2 oz) suet
- 100 g (4 oz) plain flour
- ½ teaspoon baking powder
- pinch of salt
- 4–5 tablespoons cold water

Serves 4–6

1. Dust the steak in the flour until it is evenly coated.

2. Next, in a large frying pan, brown the steak in oil. Do this in small batches, or the oil will not be hot enough to brown the meat properly.

3. Transfer the steak into the slow cooker, then add the onions. Add a little of the stout to the frying pan, scraping up all of the residue from the bottom of the pan. This will add flavour and help to thicken the casserole. Add this to the slow cooker.

4. Add the rest of the stout and the water / stock to the cooker. Simmer and add the bay leaves, mushrooms and carrot.

5. Cook on high for 3–4 hours or on low for 7–8 hours, until the steak is soft.

6. For the dumplings, mix together the suet, flour, baking powder and salt. Add 4–5 tablespoons of cold water and mix until soft and slightly sticky. Roll into balls about the size of walnuts and remove to a plate.

7. In the last hour, remove the cover from the slow cooker and add the dumplings. Re-cover and continue to cook for the remaining time or until the sauce thickens to a nice consistency.

Serve with mashed potatoes and spring greens.

Chilli Con Carne

Chilli Con Carne

A classic dish that should grace the table of every household. Easy to make, chilli con carne improves the longer it is cooked and is perfect when served with jacket potatoes.

You will need:

- 1 tablespoon oil
- 1 onion, finely chopped
- 5 or 6 garlic gloves, crushed
- 1 teaspoon ground cumin
- 1 teaspoon chilli powder
- 450 g (1 lb) beef mince
- 400 g (14 oz) canned chopped tomatoes
- 3 tablespoons tomato purée
- 1 red bell pepper, diced
- 1 green bell pepper, diced
- 4 / 5 green chillies, to taste
- 400 g (14 oz) canned kidney beans, drained
- 300 ml (10 fl. oz) cold water

Serves 4–6

1. Heat the oil in a large saucepan and fry the onion and garlic over a medium heat until softened. Add the cumin and chilli powder, stir, and fry for a moment or two, then add the beef mince and brown it all over.

2. Transfer this mixture to the slow cooker and add the canned tomatoes and the tomato purée.

Bring to a simmer and add the peppers, chillies, kidney beans and cold water.

3. Cover and cook on high for 4–5 hours or on low for 8–10 hours.

Serve with jacket potatoes or rice with sour cream, grated cheese and salad.

> **Top Tip!**
> Chilli con carne freezes well, so cook a larger batch and store some for later. This can then be defrosted and heated up for a quick and tasty meal.

Osso Buco

Osso Buco

Originally from Milan, Italy, the name osso buco means 'bone with a hole'. Packed full of flavour, these veal shanks will make a great impression when cooking for family or friends.

You will need:

- 6 pieces of osso buco, ask the butcher for cuts of equal size
- 2 tablespoons flour, seasoned with salt and black pepper
- 2 tablespoons oil
- 3 celery sticks, trimmed and chopped
- 6 carrots, peeled and chopped into large chunks
- 2 onions, peeled and finely sliced
- 4 cloves of garlic, peeled and crushed
- 1 bunch of marjoram
- 1 bunch of flat-leaf parsley
- 4 fresh bay leaves
- 400 g (14 oz) canned chopped tomatoes
- 750 ml (25 fl. oz) dry white wine

Serves 6

1. Tie the shanks with kitchen string to keep the meat together during cooking. Then, roll the shanks in the seasoned flour.

2. Next, heat the oil in a large frying pan and brown the shanks on both sides. Then, transfer the shanks to the slow cooker and add the remaining ingredients.

3. Cover and cook on low for 6–8 hours or on high for 4–5 hours, until the meat is tender.

4. Place the meat on a serving rack and spoon the sauce around and over the shanks.

Traditionally, osso buco is served with risotto alla milanese, a risotto enhanced with saffron threads. The combination of the thick sauce and buttery rice can be too rich for some tastes, so it could also be served with a leafy green salad or spinach.

Poultry

Poultry is a fantastic choice for slow cooking – it is not only widely available, but also inexpensive, versatile, and lean and healthy. Although it should not be cooked as long as other meats, slow cooked poultry has an incredible intensity of flavour that will be enjoyed by children and adults alike.

Pollo Alla Cacciatora (Hunters' Chicken)

Pollo Alla Cacciatora (Hunters' Chicken)

Cacciatora means 'hunters' in Italian. Living up to its name, this hearty dish is simple to make and is great for using up spare vegetables. A thoroughly satisfying slow cooked dish!

- 2 tablespoons oil
- 1 kg (2 lb, 2 oz) chicken pieces
- 1 green pepper, chopped
- 2 small onions, sliced
- 2 cloves garlic, chopped
- 100 g (4 oz) mushrooms, sliced
- 1 cinnamon stick
- 60 ml (2 fl. oz) dry sherry
- 400 g (14 oz) canned chopped tomatoes
- salt and pepper to season
- 3 tablespoons flour
- 3 tablespoons water

Serves 6

1. Heat the oil in a large saucepan and fry the chicken pieces, until browned.

2. Next, place the peppers, onions and garlic into the slow cooker. Add the chicken pieces and pour in the mushrooms, cinnamon stick, sherry and tomatoes. Stir well and season.

3. Cover and cook on low for 5–8 hours, or on high for 3–4 hours.

4. Remove the chicken pieces and keep warm. Make a smooth paste of flour and water, and stir into the slow cooker.

5. Return the chicken, cover and cook on a high setting for 15–20 minutes or until the sauce has thickened.

Remove the cinnamon stick and serve with hot noodles or fluffy rice.

Chicken Stroganoff

Chicken Stroganoff

Stroganoff is a dish that has roots in 19th century Russia. Why not double the ingredients of this slow cooked variant of the classic dish and freeze what you don't need for next time?

You will need:

- 2 tablespoons olive oil
- 1 small onion, finely sliced
- 500 g (1 lb, 1 oz) chicken pieces
- 225 g (8 oz) mushrooms, sliced
- 100 ml (3 fl. oz) chicken stock
- 2 tablespoons brandy
- 100 g (4 oz) crème fraiche
- 2 teaspoons of paprika
- salt and pepper to season
- small bunch of fresh chives, chopped

Serves 4

1. Heat the oil in a large frying pan and fry the onion for 2–3 minutes. Then, add the chicken pieces and brown all over.

2. Transfer the chicken and onions to the slow cooker and add the mushrooms, stock and brandy. Next, stir in the crème fraiche, paprika, salt, pepper and chives. Cover and cook on low for 5–6 hours or on high for 3–4 hours, until the chicken is tender but not overdone.

3. Remove from the heat and serve immediately with rice.

Chicken Curry

Chicken Curry

This chicken curry is so good you'll be dishing out seconds! Fantastic for the family or as a dinner party meal, this recipe is sure to become a firm favourite!

You will need:

- 2 tablespoons oil
- 2 kg (4 lb, 4 oz) chicken breast fillets or thighs, cut into pieces
- 1 green pepper, chopped
- 1 onion, chopped
- 400 g (14 oz) canned chopped tomatoes
- 1 tablespoon ground coriander
- 1½ teaspoons paprika
- 2 teaspoons fresh ginger, grated
- 1 teaspoon salt
- ½ teaspoon crushed red chilli
- ½ teaspoon ground turmeric
- ½ teaspoon ground cinnamon
- ½ teaspoon ground cloves
- 250 ml (8 fl. oz) chicken stock
- 4 teaspoons cornflour
- 2 tablespoons cold water

Serves 6

1. Heat the oil in a large saucepan and fry the chicken pieces, until browned.

2. Next, place the pepper and onion into the slow cooker and place the chicken on top of the vegetables.

3. In a bowl, combine the tomatoes, coriander, paprika, ginger, salt, chilli, turmeric, cinnamon and cloves and finally stir in the chicken stock. Then, pour over the chicken pieces.

4. Cover and cook on low for 5–6 hours or on high for 2–3 hours.

5. In the last thirty minutes of cooking time, combine the cornflour and cold water in a bowl, and then stir into the slow cooker. Cover and cook for a further 15–20 minutes on a high-heat setting, or until the sauce has thickened.

Serve with pilau rice and naan bread.

Coq au Vin

Coq au Vin

This traditional French dish, translated as 'rooster in wine', was originally a simple meal eaten by French peasants. Some people believe that its origins extend back to Julius Caesar!

You will need:

- 1 medium whole chicken
- half a bottle of red wine (a quarter to marinade)
- 4 garlic cloves, crushed
- 6 black peppercorns
- 2 bay leaves
- sprig of thyme
- 1 tablespoon olive oil
- 150 g (5 oz) pancetta
- 60 ml (2 fl. oz) cognac
- 450 g (1 lb) small baby onions, peeled but left whole
- 2 carrots, diced
- 100 g (4 oz) button mushrooms
- 200 ml (7 fl. oz) chicken stock
- salt and pepper to season

Coq au Vin

Serves 6–8

1. Cut the chicken into eight pieces (you will need a good knife, or you can ask your butcher to do it for you). From the bottom of the breastbone, cut through the backbone to separate the legs from the rest of the chicken. Cut the legs into separate drumsticks and thighs. Separate the breasts by cutting down along the breastbone, then cut each breast in two. Alternatively, you can just buy ready-cut portions.

2. Place in a non-metallic bowl, and add quarter of a bottle of the wine, 2 cloves of crushed garlic, peppercorns, bay leaves and thyme. Marinate in the refrigerator overnight.

3. Cook the pancetta in a large frying pan, before removing and browning the chicken in the bacon juices. After the chicken has browned, pour cognac over it and ignite with a match. **Use extreme caution when igniting alcohol – stand back and always have proper fire safety equipment to hand.** Move the frying pan back and forth a few times until the flames die.

4. Put the onions, garlic, carrots and mushrooms into the slow cooker, as well as the marinade juices. Next, add the chicken, pancetta and any leftover juices from the frying pan. Add the remaining ingredients, except for the wine, and pour over the chicken.

5. Cover and cook on low for 6–8 hours. After the elapsed time, turn heat to high and add the wine. Cook for an additional hour.

Serve with creamy mashed potatoes.

Confit of Duck

Confit of Duck

Confit means to slowly cook food, which is immersed in a substance for flavour and preservation. It is one of the oldest ways to preserve food, and is a speciality of south-western France.

You will need:

- 100 g (4 oz) sea salt
- 25 g (1 oz) crushed pepper
- 1 tablespoon chopped thyme
- 2 cloves garlic, crushed
- 4 duck legs
- 500 ml (17 fl. oz) goose or duck fat (approx)
- 1 teaspoon brown sugar
- 2 tablespoons soy sauce

Serves 4

1. Mix together the salt, pepper, thyme and garlic.

2. Place the duck legs in a bowl and cover with the mix. Cover and leave to cure in the refrigerator for 5–7 hours.

3. Rinse the legs and pat dry. Place the legs in the slow cooker and cover with the duck or goose fat. Cover and cook on low for 3–4 hours or until the duck is tender.

4. Allow the duck to cool (it can be kept covered in the fat in the fridge for 3–4 days). 20 minutes before you are ready to serve, heat the oven to 220°C, dissolve the sugar in the soy sauce, remove the duck from the fat and paint with the soy mix. Roast the legs for 10–12 minutes in the oven until the skin is crispy.

Serve with a light summer salad.

Pork

Pork is one of the most versatile meats to use with your slow cooker, as it comes in a variety of cuts, which are relatively inexpensive. Similarly to other meats, slow cooking pork will transform even the cheapest and toughest cuts, such as shoulder and collar. When buying pork, look for cuts that are a healthy pink colour, not grey or red. For higher welfare standards, look for The Quality Standard Mark with its distinctive Union flag logo.

Pork and Potato Hotpot

Pork and Potato Hotpot

Hotpots are traditional English dishes and were originally inspired out of necessity, with readily available ingredients. This rustic pork and potato hotpot is sure to become a family favourite.

You will need:

- 1 tablespoon oil
- 1 large onion, thinly sliced
- 1 teaspoon mixed herbs
- 2 garlic cloves, crushed
- 4 pork chops, cut into chunks
- 1 yellow pepper, sliced
- 225 g (8 oz) button mushrooms
- 900 g (2 lb) potatoes, thinly sliced
- salt and pepper to season
- 750 ml (25 fl. oz) vegetable or chicken stock

Serves 4

1. Heat the oil in a frying pan, add the onions, mixed herbs and garlic and gently cook for about 5 minutes, or until the onions are translucent. Add the pork and fry until browned.

2. Spoon the peppers, mushrooms and the onion, herbs and garlic into the slow cooker, then add the potato slices. Season with salt and pepper.

3. Next, add the pork, then pour the stock over to cover the ingredients.

4. Cover and cook the hotpot on high for 3–4 hours or until the pork and potatoes are tender.

Serve with red cabbage and rice or fresh, crusty bread.

> **Top Tip!**
> For an extra kick, why not add some whole red chillies?

Sausage Casserole

Sausage Casserole

Sausages are one of the ultimate convenience foods, and there is an increasing range of good-quality sausages available these days. This wholesome casserole is a great winter-warmer!

You will need:

- 1 tablespoon oil
- 8 good-quality sausages, cut into chunks
- 1 medium onion, diced
- 150 g (5 oz) whole baby carrots
- 3 large potatoes, cut into pieces
- 400 g (14 oz) canned kidney beans, drained
- 100 g (4 oz) green beans
- 150 g (5 oz) button mushrooms
- 500 ml (17 fl. oz) chicken stock
- squirt of tomato purée
- 150 ml (5 fl. oz) red wine
- 2 bay leaves
- cornflour to thicken

Serves 4

1. Heat the oil in the frying pan on a medium heat. Add the sausages and gently brown them.

2. Next, place all of the ingredients into the slow cooker, except for the cornflour.

3. Cover and cook on low for 6–8 hours.

4. When ready to serve, mix a couple of tablespoons of cornflour with some water in a bowl, then pour the mixture into the casserole. Remove everything from the slow cooker and simmer on the stove until the sauce is the required thickness.

Serve with fresh, crusty bread or with mashed potatoes and vegetables.

Variation – Try this recipe with Mexican sausages, adding chilli to the casserole to complement the spices in the sausage; or use Toulouse sausage, with added garlic. Whatever sausage you choose, try to adapt the recipe to complement the flavour of the sausage.

Pork Cassoulet

Pork Cassoulet

There are many versions of this dish, which originates in the south of France. Cassoulet gets its name from a cassole, the deep round earthenware pot with slanting sides in which cassoulet is ideally cooked.

You will need:

- 3 tablespoons olive oil, plus extra for drizzling
- 4 middle neck pork chops, about 500 g (1 lb, 1 oz)
- 4 pork sausages, cut into chunks
- 2 pork belly steaks, about 350 g (12 oz)
- 200 g (7 oz) mushrooms, sliced
- 4 onions, chopped
- 2 carrots, cut in half
- 2 celery sticks, washed and chopped
- 500 ml (17 fl. oz) water
- 300 ml (10 fl. oz) dry white wine
- 8 bay leaves
- 4 sprigs fresh thyme
- 8 cloves
- 8 garlic cloves
- 10 tomatoes, skinned, deseeded and roughly chopped
- 2 tablespoons sun-dried tomato purée
- salt and pepper to season
- 1 kg (2 lb, 2 oz) pre-soaked flageolet and haricot beans

Serves 6–8

1. Heat the oil in a large frying pan and brown all of the meat, before transferring it to the slow cooker.

2. Add the vegetables to the cooker, then cover the ingredients with the water and wine, plus the herbs, cloves, garlic, tomato purée and seasoning. Cook on low for 8–10 hours or on high for 4–5 hours. Add the beans 30 minutes before the end of the cooking time.

Serve with warm French bread.

Variation – This basic recipe can be used for any type of cassoulet. Instead of pork you could use lamb heart, beef shin (add dumplings an hour before the end) or duck legs. You can use any chunky cut vegetables instead of the carrot, such as swede, turnip or squash, and the longer the cooking time, the more the meat and vegetables will cook down and enhance the dish.

Thai-Style Pork Belly

Thai-Style Pork Belly

Traditional English pork gets a Thai-style makeover with this recipe. Slow cooking pork belly produces mouth-watering results – combined with sweet and tangy Thai ingredients, this dish is a winner.

You will need:

- ½ tablespoon white peppercorns
- 1 tablespoon coriander roots (if unavailable, use the stem)
- 1 garlic clove, crushed
- 2 tablespoons ground nut oil
- 450 g (1 lb) pork belly with skin, cut into thick pieces
- 4 tablespoons fish sauce
- 2 tablespoons light soy sauce
- 3 star anise
- 4 tablespoons palm sugar (if unavailable, use dark brown sugar)
- 750 ml (25 fl. oz) water
- 1 spring onion, chopped

Serves 4

1. Using a mortar and pestle or a food processor, grind the white peppercorns, coriander roots and garlic into a fine paste.

2. Next, heat a frying pan with oil and lightly brown the pork belly over a medium heat. Remove from the pan and transfer to a slow cooker.

3. Add the juices from the pan and the remaining ingredients to the slow cooker. Stir the mixture so the pork belly is covered by the liquid.

4. Cover and cook on low for 8–9 hours or on high for 4–5 hours.

Serve with rice or noodles and pak choi.

Pork and Vegetables in Cider

Pork and Vegetables in Cider

Pork and apples are a classic, timeless combination; in this recipe, the apple flavour comes from the cider, which makes a wonderful sauce.

You will need:

- 900 g (2 lb) pork steaks or pork chops
- 2 pork sausages, cut into chunks
- 1 tablespoon oil
- 1 onion, sliced
- 1 tablespoon flour
- 425 ml (14 fl. oz) dry cider
- 400 g (14 oz) canned chopped tomatoes
- 2 tablespoons tomato purée
- 1 head of broccoli, chopped
- 1 carrot, chopped
- 100 g (4 oz) sprouts, washed and prepared
- 100 g (4 oz) mushrooms, sliced
- 1 whole red chilli
- 2 bay leaves
- 1 star anise (optional)
- 2 red or green bell peppers, sliced
- salt and pepper to season

Serves 4–6

1. In a large frying pan on a medium heat, brown the pork steaks or chops and the sausages in the oil. Add the onion and the flour and stir constantly for a couple of minutes.

2. Transfer the pork and the sausages, onions and any juices to the slow cooker, before adding the cider, chopped tomatoes, tomato purée, vegetables, chilli, bay leaves and star anise.

3. Cook on high for 2–3 hours or on low for 4–5 hours, until the pork is tender.

4. In the last hour, add the peppers and season with salt and pepper, if required.

Serve with rice or fresh, crusty bread.

Italian Meatball Stew

Italian Meatball Stew

In Italy, meatballs are known as 'polpette' and are generally eaten as a main course or in a soup. This slow cooked meatball stew is rich and satisfying in flavour.

You will need:

- 340 g (12 oz) extra lean beef mince
- 2 eggs, beaten
- 50 g (2 oz) fine dry breadcrumbs
- 60 ml (2 fl. oz) milk
- 2 tablespoons grated parmesan cheese
- salt and pepper to season
- 1 teaspoon garlic powder
- 4 carrots, peeled and sliced
- 450 g (1 lb) potatoes, chopped
- 300 ml (10 fl. oz) water
- $\frac{1}{2}$ teaspoon oregano
- $\frac{1}{2}$ teaspoon basil
- 300 ml (10 fl. oz) beef stock
- 450 g (1 lb) vegetables, including courgettes and red and yellow peppers, sliced

Serves 4

1. Mix the first seven ingredients together in a large bowl. Scoop the mixture together to form firm meatballs and set aside on a plate, in the fridge.

2. Next, brown the meatballs in a frying pan, then place the carrots and potatoes in the slow cooker and place the meatballs on top.

3. Combine the water, oregano, basil, beef stock, and pour over the meatballs.

4. Cover and cook on low for 4–6 hours. Add the vegetables and turn the slow cooker to high. Cover and continue to cook for another hour, or until the vegetables are tender.

Serve piping hot with fresh, crusty bread.

Lamb / Mutton

Lamb has traditionally been linked to roasts and barbecues, but it really comes into its own when it's slow cooked. The results are mouth-watering, tender and full-flavoured. Lambs' peak season and widest availability is April through to September. When buying lamb, look for cuts that are lean and firm, with creamy-white fat. Lamb shanks and knuckles are perfect for slow cooking – the meat falls off the bone! Underrated mutton cuts are similar to lamb, but tend to be larger, darker in colour and have a richer flavour that is almost 'gamey' in taste.

Honey Lamb Shanks

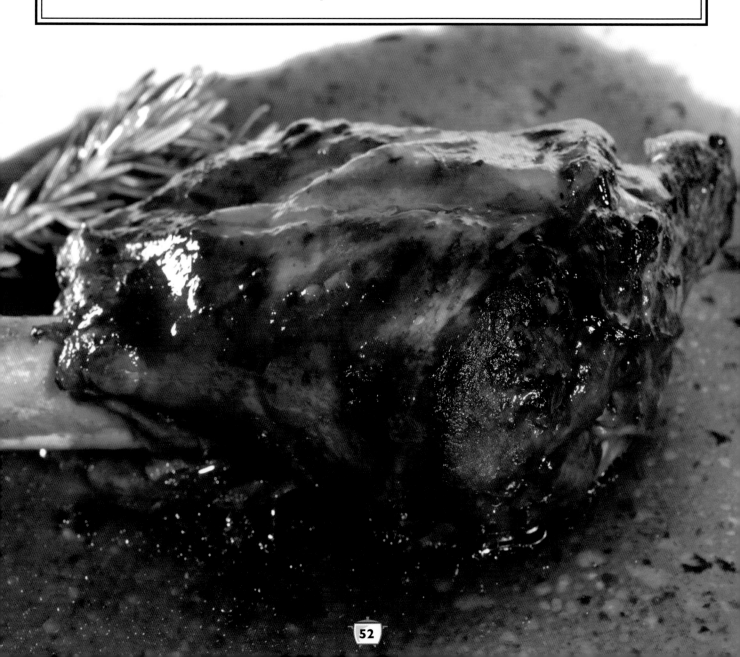

Honey Lamb Shanks

These glazed honey shanks are delicious – the meat falls off the bone. Perfect for parties, this dish will appeal to the sophisticated guest.

You will need:

- 50 g (2 oz) butter
- 4 lamb shanks
- 6 shallots or 2 onions, peeled and sliced into rings
- 5 cloves of garlic, crushed

- 1 orange, juiced (grate the rind and set it aside)
- 250 ml (8 fl. oz) red wine
- 1 tablespoon Worcestershire sauce
- 2 tablespoons honey
- 2 teaspoons cayenne pepper (can substitute with chilli powder)
- rosemary, a few fresh sprigs
- salt and pepper to season

Serves 4

Honey Lamb Shanks

1. Melt the butter in a frying pan on a medium heat. Add the lamb shanks and brown them all over.

2. After the lamb shanks have browned, leave the juices in the frying pan and add the shanks to the slow cooker. Place the fresh rosemary on top of them.

3. Sauté the orange rind, the garlic and the onions in the juices left from browning the lamb. Next, add the red wine, Worcestershire sauce, honey, cayenne pepper, chicken stock and salt and pepper to the frying pan. Stir the ingredients and bring them to a simmer for about 5 minutes. When finished, pour the sauce over the lamb shanks in the slow cooker and cook on low for 6–7 hours.

4. After the allotted cooking time, remove the cover from the slow cooker and increase the heat level to high. Continue to cook the lamb shanks and honey for another hour and a half so that the orange and honey sauce can thicken. Stir from time to time if you need to.

5. To serve the honey lamb shanks, remove them from the slow cooker and scoop equal amounts of the orange honey sauce from the cooker onto the lamb.

Serve with rice and a fresh salad.

Classic Irish Stew

Classic Irish Stew

Made with lamb, mutton or beef, Irish stew ('Stobhach Gaelach' in Irish) is a simple, traditional and inexpensive stew that is perfect for slow cooking.

You will need:

- 50 g (2 oz) butter
- 2 kg (4 lb, 4 oz) stewing mutton or lamb
- 3 onions, peeled and thickly sliced
- 900 g (2 lb) potatoes, peeled and thickly sliced
- 450 g (1 lb) carrots, cut into thick chunks
- 450 g (1 lb) turnips, peeled and cut into large chunks
- 2 bay leaves and 2 sprigs of rosemary
- 2 teaspoons Worcestershire sauce (or to taste)
- salt and pepper to season
- 1 litre (34 fl. oz) beef stock (or water)
- 900 g (2 lb) potatoes, peeled and thickly sliced
- 1 sprig parsley, chopped

Serves 6–8

1. Melt the butter in a frying pan on a medium heat. Add the meat and brown, then remove from the pan. Soften the onions in the same pan.

2. Transfer the meat and onions to the slow cooker, along with any juices from the frying pan. Add the potatoes, carrots, turnips, bay leaves, rosemary, Worcestershire Sauce, seasoning and enough stock or water to cover the ingredients.

3. Cover and cook on low for 6–7 hours, or until the meat is tender and the potatoes are soft.

Serve scattered with plenty of chopped parsley.

Mutton Shanks with Red Wine Sauce

Mutton Shanks with Red Wine Sauce

Mutton has suffered a bad reputation in British cooking in recent years, but it is a delicious and tender meat, and is perfect for slow cooking.

You will need:

- 4 x 340 g (12 oz) mutton shanks
- 100 g (4 oz) plain flour, seasoned
- 4 tablespoons cep powder
- 50 g (2 oz) butter
- 375 ml (12 fl. oz) madeira
- 500 ml (17 fl. oz) red wine
- 2 large oranges, zest and juice
- 500 ml (17 fl. oz) lamb stock
- 1 bunch thyme
- 1 bunch parsley

Serves 4

1. Dust the mutton shanks with the seasoned flour and cep powder.

2. Heat the butter in a large frying pan and lightly brown the mutton shanks on all sides. Remove and put to one side.

3. Tip the fat from the frying pan into the slow cooker, then add the madeira, wine, orange zest and juice and the lamb stock.

4. Put the shanks into the slow cooker with the thyme and season. Cover and cook on high for 2–3 hours or on low for 5–6 hours.

5. Once cooked, remove the mutton from the slow cooker, skim the excess fat off the sauce, leave the lid off the cooker and reduce the cooking liquid by half for about 10 minutes. Once reduced, turn off the heat, put the mutton back into the liquid so that it stays warm and cooks to a glaze.

Serve with creamy mashed potatoes and green vegetables.

Moroccan Lamb Stew

Moroccan Lamb Stew

Moroccan cuisine is a blend of African, Arabian and European influences. The food of this nation is characterised by subtle scents, delicate flavours and great presentation.

You will need:

- 100 g (4 oz) dried whole apricots, halved
- 3 tablespoons olive oil
- 1.5 kg (3 lb, 3 oz) diced leg of lamb
- 1 large onion, finely chopped
- 1 green pepper, sliced
- 2 garlic cloves, crushed
- 1 teaspoon ground cumin
- 1 teaspoon ground coriander
- 1 teaspoon ground cinnamon
- 400 g (14 oz) canned chopped tomatoes
- 300 ml (10 fl. oz) lamb stock
- pinch saffron threads
- salt and pepper to season
- 3 tablespoons ground almonds
- 1 butternut squash, peeled and diced
- 4 tomatoes, skinned and quartered
- 2 tablespoons harissa (optional)
- 450 g (1 lb) couscous, prepared as directed on the packet

Serves 6

1. Place the apricots in a bowl and cover with 150 ml (5 fl. oz) boiling water. Leave to soak for

2 hours.
2. Heat the olive oil in a large frying pan and brown the lamb in batches, then set aside. Add the onion and cook gently for 10 minutes until soft and golden. Add the garlic and spices and cook for a further 2 minutes, then add to the slow cooker.

3. Next, add the lamb to the slow cooker, along with the apricots and their soaking liquid, the canned tomatoes and stock. Stir in the saffron, salt and ground almonds. Cover and cook on low for 3–4 hours.

4. Add the squash, peppers, tomatoes and harissa with a little extra water, if necessary, and cook on low for a further hour or until the squash is tender.

5. Season to taste, adding extra harissa if desired.

Serve with couscous.

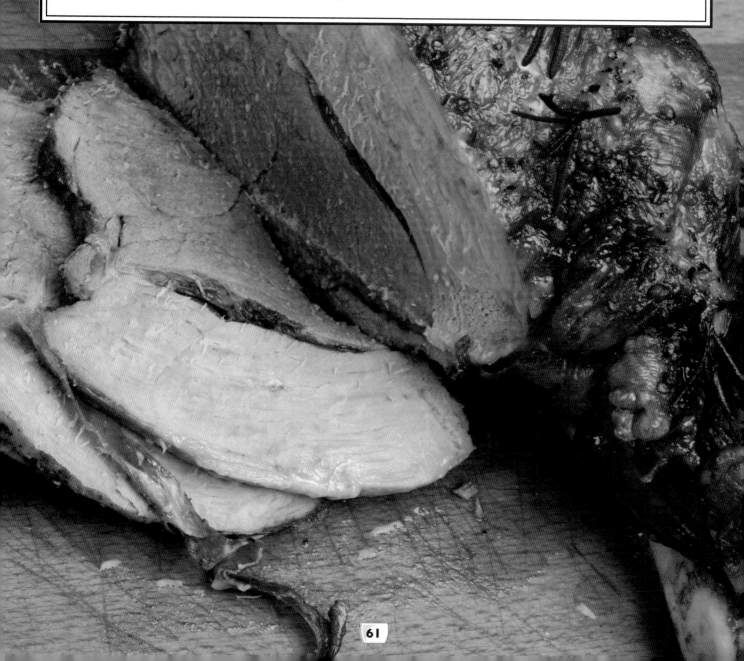

Leg of Lamb

Leg of Lamb

Slow cooking a whole leg of lamb guarantees succulence and the vegetables cooked alongside the meat absorb the glorious flavours.

You will need:

- 1 leg of lamb (about 2.5 kg or 5 lb)
- 5 cloves of garlic, peeled and sliced
- 2 tablespoons fresh or dried rosemary
- salt and pepper to season
- 2 tablespoons olive oil
- 1 onion, sliced
- 1 carrot, chopped into thick chunks
- 1 parsnip, chopped into thick chunks
- 1 litre (34 fl. oz) vegetable stock
- 60 ml (2 fl. oz) low salt soy sauce

Serves 6

1. With a sharp knife, cut small slits into the leg of lamb at random spots around the whole piece of meat. Place a slice of garlic in each slit. Chop the rosemary and rub the leg of lamb with it, then season well.

2. Heat the oil in a large frying pan and brown the lamb on all sides. Next, add the vegetables to the slow cooker and pour the vegetable stock and the soy sauce over them. When the lamb is browned, put it into the cooker on top of the vegetables.

3. Cover the slow cooker and cook the lamb for 6–7 hours on low. Before serving, take the leg of lamb out of the slow cooker and let it rest on a rack for about 20 minutes. It will then be ready for carving. You can use the remaining juices in the cooker as gravy and freeze any that is left-over for future meals.

Serve with the vegetables in the slow cooker, along with roast potatoes and mint or redcurrent jelly.

Fish

Seafood and fish can be cooked in slow cookers, but due to the delicate nature of the flesh, seafood tends to take a shorter time of 2–5 hours. Make sure you serve your seafood dish as soon as it's ready to avoid drying out. When buying fish, purchase those that are ethically sourced and try to keep up to date with which fish are sustainable. Vary the type of fish that you buy – this not only guarantees an exciting and unpredictable menu, but it helps to take the pressue off over-fished species.

Seafood Chowder

Seafood Chowder

Chowder has its origins in the fishing villages along the north and west coasts of France and in Cornwall. When fishermen returned with their catch, villages had a pot waiting for a portion of fish, to be served later as part of the community's welcoming celebration.

You will need:

- 450 g (1 lb) haddock fillets, or other firm fresh fish, free from bones and skin
- 250 g (9 oz) potatoes, peeled and diced
- 1 stick of celery, chopped finely

- 1 onion, chopped
- 1 tablespoon dried parsley
- 1 tablespoon dried rosemary, crushed
- salt and pepper to season
- Tabasco or other hot sauce to taste
- 500 ml (17 fl. oz) white wine
- 250 ml (8 fl. oz) fish stock
- 375 g (12 oz) mixed shellfish – mussels, clams, shrimps or prawns
- 100 ml (3 fl. oz) double cream
- 3 tablespoons melted butter
- 3 tablespoons plain flour

Seafood Chowder

Serves 6

Note: You can add just about any type of seafood to this recipe to suit your tastes; clams, shrimp, scallops, etc. Additionally, you can add some sweetcorn if you like. If you like a little extra spice, try a dash or two of chilli powder.

1. Cut the fish fillets into pieces, then place them into the slow cooker, along with the potatoes, celery and onion.

2. Add the parsley, rosemary and salt and pepper to season. Gently mix them in with the fish.

3. Add the hot sauce to taste, along with the white wine and fish stock.

4. Stir gently again, then cover and cook on high for 4 hours or on low for 8 hours.

5. About an hour before your seafood chowder is finished cooking add the mixed shellfish. Next, blend together the cream, melted butter and the flour, making sure it is mixed well. Gently stir it into the chowder and continue to cook.

Serve with fresh bread.

Jambalaya

Jambalaya

Jambalaya is a rice dish from the southern states of America, and an example of how French settlers in that part of the US have influenced the national cuisine.

You will need:

- 2 tablespoons oil
- 175 g (6 oz) chicken breasts or thighs, diced
- 175 g (6 oz) chorizo or spiced sausage, sliced
- 1 onion, finely chopped
- 4 garlic cloves, crushed
- 50 g (2 oz) okra, sliced
- 2 red or green peppers, diced
- 1 teaspoon paprika
- 1 teaspoon cayenne
- ½ teaspoon cumin
- 425 ml (14 fl. oz) chicken stock
- 1 bay leaf
- 175 g (6 oz) shrimps, prawns or mussels
- 450 g (1 lb) long grain rice

Serves 2–4

1. Heat a frying pan with the oil and add the chicken and sausage. Brown the meat all over before transferring it to the slow cooker.

2. Next, add the onion, garlic, okra and peppers to the cooker. Season with paprika, cayenne and cumin, pour over the chicken stock and add the bay leaf.

3. Cover, and cook on low for 7–8 hours or on high for 3–4 hours. Stir in the shrimps, prawns or mussels during the last 30 minutes of cooking time.

4. Cook the long grain rice, according to the packet instructions. Ten minutes before serving, stir the rice into the jambalaya mixture so it absorbs the wonderful flavours.

Serve with salad and warm, crusty French bread.

Top Tip!
If you are in the mood for a bit more spice, add a few drops of Tabasco sauce!

Classic Bouillabaisse

Classic Bouillabaisse

Traditionally, the French serve Bouillabaise in two courses: the soup first and then the fish. However, it is just as good when the fish and soup are served together.

You will need:

- 2 leeks, washed and sliced lengthways
- 8 sprigs fresh tarragon
- 8 fresh sprigs flat-leaf parsley
- $\frac{1}{2}$ teaspoon coriander seeds
- $\frac{1}{2}$ teaspoon fennel seeds
- $\frac{1}{2}$ teaspoon cumin seeds
- 1 teaspoon tomato purée
- 400 g (14 oz) canned whole plum tomatoes
- 2 tablespoons olive oil
- 2 small onions, peeled and diced
- 4 cloves garlic, crushed
- 1 teaspoon sweet paprika
- 8 sun-dried tomatoes (dry, not packed in oil)
- 1 teaspoon saffron strands
- $\frac{1}{2}$ teaspoon turmeric
- 2 teaspoons harissa (optional)
- 1.25 kg (3 lb) fish heads and bone (use fish, such as sole, snapper, or bass), washed and prepared
- 6 dried fennel branches
- peel from 3 oranges
- salt and pepper to season
- 3 lobsters (optional)
- 1.25 kg (3 lb) mussels, scrubbed and beards trimmed
- 2 kg (4 lb, 4 oz) fish fillets, such as halibut, red snapper, and monkfish, cut into pieces.

Serves 6–8

1. Begin by making a bouquet garni. Cut dark-green leek leaves into two equal lengths. Arrange the tarragon and parsley sprigs in the centre of one leaf. Place the other leaf on top to enclose the tarragon and tie with kitchen string.

2. Next, heat a frying pan over a medium heat and add the coriander, fennel and cumin seeds. Cook for 2–3 minutes, shaking the pan or stirring frequently, until toasted and fragrant. Let the seeds cool in a bowl.

Top Tip!
You can add just about any type of seafood to this recipe to suit your tastes.

Classic Bouillabaisse

3. Strain the can of plum tomatoes over a small bowl, reserving the liquid, but discarding the seeds. Place the tomatoes in a bowl with the liquid and set aside.

4. Heat the oil in a large frying pan and add the onions, garlic, and paprika. Cook until the onions become translucent. Next, add the tomato purée, whole plum tomatoes and their liquid, sun-dried tomatoes, saffron, turmeric, harissa and the toasted coriander, fennel and cumin seeds. Stir to combine.

5. Transfer the mixture to the slow cooker and add the fish heads and bones. Then, add the fennel, orange peel, and bouquet garni. Add enough water to just cover the fish and season. Next, skim the foam from the surface, reduce the heat and cook on low for 3–4 hours. Then, pour the stock through a sieve into a large bowl and discard solids. Return the liquid to the slow cooker and season.

6. Meanwhile, bring a large pan of cold water to a boil. Quickly add the lobster and cook for about 12 minutes. Remove the pan from heat, drain the lobster and submerge in cold water to stop cooking. Drain again.

7. Add 250 ml (8 fl. oz) of the fish stock from the slow cooker into a large saucepan and add the same amount of water. Bring to a boil and add the mussels. Cover the pan and cook until the mussels open. Remove from the heat and discard any mussels that do not open.

8. Meanwhile, add the fish fillets to the slow cooker and cook until they are cooked through. Remove the tails and claws from the cooked lobster and crack them open, adding the meat and the mussels to the slow cooker, just long enough to warm.

Serve with rouille and crunchy French bread.

Game

Game has a long history in Britain and has recently become more popular due to its increased availability. Game meat falls into two categories – feathered (pigeon, pheasant, grouse, etc.) and furred (rabbit, venison, hare, etc.) Older game works best for slow cooking, as it is tougher and therefore requires a longer cooking time.

Pheasant and Venison Casserole

Pheasant and Venison Casserole

Readily available throughout the entire shooting season, pheasant and venison, combined with the chestnuts, create a rich winter dish.

You will need:

- 450 g (1 lb) lean boneless venison, cubed
- 1 large pheasant, jointed
- 2 tablespoons fine oatmeal
- 2 tablespoons olive oil
- 300 ml (10 fl. oz) red wine
- 2 onions, finely chopped
- 150 ml (5 fl. oz) port
- 425 ml (14 fl. oz) beef stock
- 1 teaspoon fresh thyme leaves
- 3 juniper berries, crushed
- 2 good pinches of allspice
- 150 g (5 oz) baby shallots, peeled
- 250 g (9 oz) mushrooms, sliced
- 250 g (9 oz) whole baby carrots, scrubbed and trimmed
- 250g (9 oz) baby parsnips, scrubbed and trimmed
- 100 g (4 oz) canned or vacuum-packed cooked chestnuts

Serves 4–6

1. To begin, toss the pieces of venison and the jointed pheasant in the oatmeal to lightly coat, then shake to remove any excess.

2. Heat the oil in a large frying pan and brown the venison and the pheasant in batches, until lightly coloured. Transfer to a plate. Add a splash of red wine to the pan and de-glaze, adding the left-over meat juices to the slow cooker.

3. Next, add the chopped onions to the slow cooker and then the remaining wine, port, stock, thyme, juniper and allspice, plus a little seasoning to taste, stirring constantly.

4. Stir in the shallots, mushrooms, whole baby carrots and parsnips, plus the venison and pheasant. Cover and cook on low for 6–7 hours or on high for 3–4, until the meat is really tender and the onions have softened.

5. When the meat is cooked, stir in the chestnuts, then taste and adjust the seasoning.

Serve with crusty French bread or mashed potatoes.

Rabbit Stew

Rabbit Stew

Once a staple food in Britain, rabbit is slowly, but surely, finding its way back onto household tables.

You will need:

- 1 rabbit (portioned), or use 4–6 butcher-prepared rabbit portions
- 100 g (4 oz) flour, to coat rabbit portions
- 1 teaspoon olive oil
- 2 onions, chopped
- 100 g (4 oz) streaky bacon, chopped into small pieces
- 300 ml (10 fl. oz) white wine
- 2 red or yellow peppers, sliced
- 100 g (4 oz) button mushrooms
- 6 garlic cloves, peeled and crushed
- 3 large tomatoes, peeled and chopped or 400 g (14 oz) canned chopped tomatoes
- 2 tablespoons tomato purée
- 1 chicken stock cube
- 2 bay leaves
- 1 pinch of mixed herbs
- 1 tablespoon of oregano
- 1 tablespoon basil

Serves 4–6

1. Roll the rabbit portions in the seasoned flour.

2. Heat the oil in a frying pan and brown the rabbit. Add the onions, bacon and garlic to the pan and fry until the onions have softened and the bacon has cooked.

3. Next, transfer the onions, bacon, garlic and rabbit, along with the frying pan juices, to the slow cooker. Pour the wine over the ingredients and add the peppers, mushrooms, tomatoes, tomato purée, stock cube, bay leaves and all of the herbs.

4. Cover and cook on low for 6–8 hours, or until the rabbit is tender.

Serve with mashed potatoes and seasonal vegetables.

Vegetables and Pulses

Substantial and satisfying, vegetable casseroles, curries and stews are great in a slow cooker. Fresh root vegetables, such as carrots, potatoes, onions, leeks, swede, parsnips, turnips, celery and celeriac are best suited to slow cooking, but other vegetables may also be used. Pulses, including beans, chickpeas and lentils are fantastic for slow cooking, but may need to be soaked overnight before cooking.

Chickpea Curry

Chickpea Curry

Chickpeas are a great slow cooking ingredient. High in protein, they are one of the oldest cultivated vegetables and work well in curries.

You will need:

- 2 tablespoons olive oil
- 2 onions, sliced
- 2 cloves garlic, crushed
- 1 teaspoon cumin powder
- 1 teaspoon coriander powder
- 1 teaspoon turmeric powder
- 5 cm (2 in.) piece root ginger, grated
- 3 green chillies, deseeded and chopped
- 1 teaspoon mustard seeds
- 400 g (14 oz) canned chickpeas, drained
- 400 g (14 oz) canned chopped tomatoes
- 1 tablespoon mild curry paste
- pinch of garam masala

Serves 2–4

1. Heat the oil in a large frying pan and cook the onions and garlic until softened. Add the mustard seeds, spices, ginger and chilli and cook for a further 30 seconds.

2. Add the fried ingredients to the slow cooker and stir in the chickpeas, chopped tomatoes and curry paste.

3. Cook for 6–9 hours. Before serving, add the garam masala.

Serve the curry with pilau rice and naan bread.

Aloo Gobi (Cauliflower and Potato Curry)

Aloo Gobi (Cauliflower and Potato Curry)

Indian cuisine is ideal for vegetarians, as a large percentage of the population do not eat meat. This recipe can be adapted to suit your own tastes, or to suit the availability of seasonal vegetables.

You will need:

- 2 tablespoons ghee or vegetable oil
- 1 large onion, sliced
- 4 / 5 garlic cloves, crushed
- 2½ cm (1 in.) root ginger, chopped
- 1 teaspoon black mustard seeds
- 1 teaspoon ground coriander
- 1 teaspoon ground cumin
- 1 teaspoon turmeric
- 1 teaspoon ground fenugreek
- 4 green cardamoms, split open and slightly crushed
- 2 green chillies, left whole
- 1 cinnamon stick
- 450 g (1 lb) potatoes, cubed
- 1 cauliflower, in florets
- 100 g (4 oz) green beans, chopped
- 400 g (14 oz) canned chopped tomatoes

Serves 2–4

1. Heat the oil in a frying pan and add the onion, frying until softened. Add the garlic, ginger, mustard seeds, ground coriander, cumin, turmeric, fenugreek, cardamoms and chillies and fry for two minutes until the spices start to smell fragrant.

2. Next, transfer all of the ingredients to the slow cooker and add the cinnamon stick, vegetables and chopped tomatoes.

3. Cover and cook on low for 6 hours or on high for 3–4 hours. The vegetables should be tender and the sauce reduced.

Remove the cinnamon stick and serve with fragrant rice, naan breads and pickles.

Bean and Barley Soup

Bean and Barley Soup

Healthy and filling, beans and barley are an excellent combination for a slow cooker. These two ingredients have been used as a staple food for hundreds of years around the world.

You will need:

- 250 g (9 oz) mixed beans
- 2 tablespoons oil
- I garlic clove, chopped
- I large onion, chopped
- 100 g (4 oz) celeriac or 2 sticks of celery, peeled and diced
- I large carrot, peeled and diced
- salt and pepper to season
- 900 ml (30 fl. oz) vegetable stock
- 125 g (5 oz) barley
- I red pepper, sliced
- I medium potato, diced

Serves 2–4

1. Prepare the mixed beans by soaking them in 500 ml (17 fl. oz) of water for 8–24 hours. Drain and place into the slow cooker.

2. Heat a tablespoon of oil in a large saucepan and add the garlic, onion and celery. Cook for a minute or two. Add the carrot and celeriac and season with salt and pepper.

3. Next, transfer the mixture into the slow cooker and stir in the stock, barley, pepper and potato.

4. Cover and cook on low for 5–6 hours, or until the beans are soft.

5. Remove half of the vegetables and beans to a blender or processor, purée and return to the pan. Add more water to produce a thickish soup.

Serve piping hot with warm, crusty bread.

Spicy Root and Lentil Casserole

Spicy Root and Lentil Casserole

Not only are lentils filling and packed with protein, they are great to use in a slow cooker. This spicy root and lentil casserole uses fragrant flavours from India – perfect for a healthy veggie supper!

You will need:

- 2 tablespoons oil
- 1 onion, chopped
- 2 garlic cloves, crushed
- 700 g (1 lb, 5 oz) potatoes, peeled and cut into chunks
- 4 carrots, thickly sliced
- 2 parsnips, thickly sliced
- 2 tablespoons curry paste or powder
- 1 litre (34 fl. oz) vegetable stock
- 100 g (4 oz) red lentils, rinsed
- a small bunch of fresh coriander, roughly chopped

Serves 2–4

1. Heat the oil in a large frying pan and cook the onion and garlic over a medium heat for a couple of minutes. Once softened, add the onions and garlic to the slow cooker.

2. Next, add the potatoes, carrots and parsnips, stir in the curry paste or powder and pour in the stock. Finally, add the lentils, cover and cook on low for 5–6 hours or until the lentils and vegetables are tender and the sauce has thickened.

3. Stir in most of the coriander, season and serve.

Serve with a sprinkle of coriander, yogurt and naan bread.

Minestrone Soup

Minestrone Soup

An Italian staple, minestrone soup was originally created as a cheap and filling dish, made from left-overs. Due to this, it is considered to be part of the 'cucina provera', an Italian term that literally means 'poor kitchen'. Today, the soup includes fresh vegetables and is made for its own sake – as a healthy and delicious dish that is perfect for slow cooking!

You will need:

- 750 ml (25 fl. oz) vegetable stock
- 400 g (14 oz) canned chopped tomatoes
- 400 g (14 oz) canned white (cannellini or navy) beans, drained
- 2 carrots, peeled and chopped
- 1 celery stalk, chopped
- 1 onion, chopped
- 25 g (1 oz) peas
- 1 teaspoon dried thyme
- ½ teaspoon dried sage
- 2 bay leaves
- salt and pepper to season
- 225 g (8 oz) cooked pasta (ditalini pasta is perfect, but other types can be used)
- 1 medium courgette, chopped

Serves 4–6

1. Simply add all of the ingredients to the slow cooker. Cover and cook on low for 6–8 hours or on high for 3–4 hours.

Top Tip!
Part of the beauty of this dish is that you can add any spare ingredients you have lying around that need to be used up.

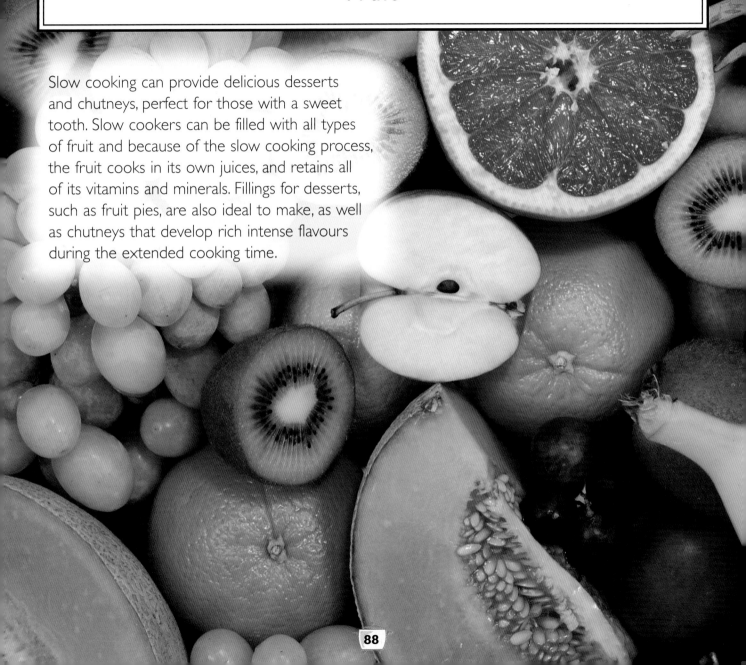

Fruit

Slow cooking can provide delicious desserts and chutneys, perfect for those with a sweet tooth. Slow cookers can be filled with all types of fruit and because of the slow cooking process, the fruit cooks in its own juices, and retains all of its vitamins and minerals. Fillings for desserts, such as fruit pies, are also ideal to make, as well as chutneys that develop rich intense flavours during the extended cooking time.

Mango and Apricot Fruit Chutney

In the 1600's, chutney was shipped to Europe as a luxury item. A delicious condiment for meat and cheese, home-made chutney is an impressive addition to any meal.

You will need:

- 450 g (1 lb) ready-to-eat apricots, chopped
- 450 g (1 lb) slightly under-ripe mangoes, peeled and diced
- 650 g (1 lb, 4 oz) light muscavado sugar
- 375 ml (12 fl. oz) cider or wine vinegar
- 2 oranges (juice and zest)
- 50 g (2 oz) ginger, peeled and finely grated
- 2 red chillies, deseeded and chopped
- $\frac{1}{2}$ teaspoon salt
- 2 tablespoons lemon juice

1. Place all of the ingredients (apart from the lemon juice) into the slow cooker, stir well and turn on high.

2. Cover and cook for 2–3 hours, stirring frequently in the first hour, until the sugar has dissolved, then stir occasionally to prevent sticking.

3. Remove the lid and continue to cook for 30–40 minutes until thick and sticky.

4. Stir in the lemon juice at the end of cooking.

Pour into a preserving jar with an air-tight lid or jar with a cover. Serve with cheese, cold meat or curries.

Recipes

Use the following pages to write down your own slow cooking recipes.

Recipes

Recipes

Recipes

Recipes

Recipes